favouri
dinners

The Family Circle® Promise of Success

Welcome to the world of Confident Cooking, created for you in the
Family Circle® Test Kitchen, where recipes are double-tested by our team
of home economists to achieve a high standard of success.

MURDOCH
B O O K S

EVERYDAY FAVOURITES

Everyone has a favourite meal, often something remembered from childhood that you always wished you had a foolproof recipe for. Now you need look no further.

SPAGHETTI BOLOGNESE

Prep time: 15 minutes
Cooking time: 2 hours
    50 minutes
Serves 4

60 g butter
1 onion, finely chopped
2 cloves garlic, crushed
1 celery stick, finely chopped
1 carrot, finely diced
50 g piece pancetta, finely diced
500 g lean beef mince
1 tablespoon chopped fresh oregano
1 cup (250 ml) red wine
2 cups (500 ml) beef stock
2 tablespoons tomato paste
2 x 400 g cans crushed tomatoes
400 g spaghetti
3 tablespoons grated reggiano Parmesan

1 Melt the butter in a large saucepan, add the onion and cook over medium heat for 2–3 minutes, or until it starts to soften. Add the garlic, celery and carrot, and cook, stirring, over low heat, for 5 minutes. Increase the heat to high, add the pancetta, beef and oregano, and cook for 4–5 minutes, or until browned. Use a fork to break up any lumps.

2 Pour in the wine, reduce the heat and simmer for 4–5 minutes, or until it is absorbed. Add the stock, tomato paste and tomato, and season well. Cover with a lid and allow the sauce to simmer for 1 1/2 hours, stirring occasionally to prevent it from catching on the bottom of the saucepan. Uncover and simmer for another hour, stirring occasionally.

3 Cook the spaghetti in a large saucepan of boiling water until *al dente*. Drain, divide among four serving plates and top with the sauce. Serve immediately, with the Parmesan.

Nutrition per serve: Fat 26 g; Protein 46 g; Carbohydrate 80 g; Dietary Fibre 7.5 g; Cholesterol 114 mg; 3265 kJ (780 Cal)

Spaghetti Bolognese

CAESAR SALAD

Prep time: 25 minutes
Cooking time: 10 minutes
Serves 4

2–3 anchovies
3 eggs
1 teaspoon Worcestershire
  sauce
3 cloves garlic, crushed
2 tablespoons lime juice
1 teaspoon Dijon mustard
3/4 cup (185 ml) olive oil
3 slices white bread, crusts
  removed
15 g butter
1 tablespoon olive oil, extra
3 rashers bacon
1 large or 4 baby cos
  lettuces, large leaves torn
3 eggs, extra, hard-boiled
  and quartered
3/4 cup (75 g) shaved
  Parmesan

1 Place the anchovies, eggs, Worcestershire sauce, garlic, lime juice and mustard in a food processor and process until smooth. With the motor running, slowly add the oil to produce a creamy dressing. Season. **2** Cut the bread into 1.5 cm cubes. Heat the butter and extra oil in a frying pan over medium heat until the butter has melted, add the bread and cook, tossing, for 4–5 minutes, or until crisp and golden.

Caesar salad (top), and Tuna bake

Remove and drain well. Cook the bacon in the same pan for 4–5 minutes, or until crisp, then break into pieces. **3** Divide the lettuce, croutons and bacon among four bowls, drizzle with the dressing and top with the eggs and Parmesan.

Nutrition per serve: Fat 66 g; Protein 26 g; Carbohydrate 8 g; Dietary Fibre 1.5 g; Cholesterol 360 mg; 3015 kJ (720 Cal)

TUNA BAKE

Prep time: 20 minutes
Cooking time: 45 minutes
Serves 6

200 g short, curly pasta
4 eggs, hard-boiled and
  roughly chopped
4 spring onions, finely
  chopped
1 tablespoon chopped
  fresh dill
1 tablespoon lemon juice
110 g butter
3 teaspoons madras curry
  powder
50 g plain flour
1 1/2 cups (375 ml) milk
1 1/2 cups (375 ml) cream
170 g whole-egg mayonnaise
3 x 210 g cans tuna, drained
2 cups (160 g) fresh white
  breadcrumbs
1 clove garlic, crushed
1 tablespoon finely chopped
  fresh flat-leaf parsley
2 tablespoons grated
  Parmesan

1 Preheat the oven to moderate 180°C (350°F/ Gas 4). Cook the pasta in a large saucepan of rapidly boiling water until *al dente*. Drain well. Lightly grease a 2 litre ovenproof dish. Combine the egg, spring onion, dill and lemon juice, and season. **2** Melt 60 g butter in a saucepan, add the curry powder and cook for 30 seconds. Stir in the plain flour and cook for 1 minute, or until foaming. Remove from the heat, gradually stir in the milk and cream, then return to low heat and stir constantly until the sauce boils and thickens. Reduce to a simmer for 1–2 minutes, then stir in the mayonnaise. Combine the sauce, cooked pasta, tuna and egg mixture, and spoon into the prepared dish. **3** Melt the remaining butter in a frying pan, add the breadcrumbs and garlic, and cook, stirring, for 1 minute, or until the crumbs are golden and coated in butter. Stir in the parsley and grated Parmesan, and sprinkle over the tuna mixture. Bake for 15–20 minutes, or until golden and heated through.

Nutrition per serve: Fat 73.5 g; Protein 26 g; Carbohydrate 48 g; Dietary Fibre 3 g; Cholesterol 339.5 mg; 3960 kJ (945 Cal)

GARLIC PRAWNS

Prep time: 30 minutes
Cooking time: 10 minutes
Serves 6 as a starter

1.5 kg medium raw prawns,
    peeled and deveined,
    tails intact
150 ml olive oil
150 g butter
10 cloves garlic, finely
    chopped
1 small fresh red chilli,
    seeded and finely chopped
3 spring onions, thinly sliced
lemon wedges, to serve

1 Cut a slit down the
back of each prawn.
Heat the oil and butter
over high heat in a large,
deep frying pan until the
butter melts. Add the
garlic and chilli, and
cook for 1–2 minutes,
or until the garlic starts
to change colour.
2 Add the prawns in
two batches, and cook
for 1–2 minutes, or
until they are pink and
cooked through. Return
all of the prawns to the
pan, with the spring
onion, and season to
taste. Divide among
warmed dishes and serve
with lemon wedges and
crusty bread.

Nutrition per serve: Fat 42.5 g;
Protein 26 g; Carbohydrate 1 g;
Dietary Fibre 1 g; Cholesterol
248 mg; 2045 kJ (490 Cal)

Note: The chilli may be omitted
for a milder flavour.

VEAL PARMIGIANA

Prep time: 25 minutes
Cooking time: 50 minutes
Serves 4

1/4 cup (60 ml) olive oil
1 clove garlic, crushed
pinch cayenne pepper
pinch caster sugar
400 g can crushed tomatoes
3 teaspoons chopped fresh
    oregano
1/3 cup (40 g) plain flour
2 eggs
2/3 cup (65 g) dry
    breadcrumbs
4 large veal cutlets, well
    trimmed
100 g mozzarella, thinly
    sliced
1/3 cup (35 g) grated
    Parmesan

1 Preheat the oven to
moderately hot 190°C
(375°F/Gas 5). Heat
1 tablespoon oil in
a small saucepan over
medium heat, add the
garlic and cook for
30 seconds. Add the
cayenne, sugar, crushed
tomatoes and half the
oregano, and cook,
stirring occasionally,
for 20 minutes, or until
thickened and pulpy.
Season well with salt
and black pepper.
2 Meanwhile, place the
flour in a wide, shallow
bowl, and season well.
Beat the eggs with
2 tablespoons of water
and pour into another
wide bowl. Combine

the breadcrumbs with
the remaining oregano,
season, and place in a
third bowl.
3 Pound the cutlets
between 2 sheets of
plastic wrap until they
are flattened to 5 mm
thick (take care not to
tear the flesh from the
bone). Coat in the
seasoned flour, shaking
off any excess, then dip
both sides in the egg
mixture, letting the
excess drip off. Press the
veal in the breadcrumbs
to coat evenly. Heat the
remaining oil in a large
frying pan. Add the
veal cutlets in two
batches and brown over
medium–high heat for
about 2 minutes on
each side. Transfer to a
shallow baking dish large
enough to fit them side
by side.
4 Spread the sauce over
each cutlet. Cover with
the mozzarella and
sprinkle with the
Parmesan. Bake for
20 minutes, or until
the cheeses have melted
and browned. Serve
immediately, with a
green salad if desired.

Nutrition per serve: Fat 26.5 g;
Protein 45 g; Carbohydrate 25 g;
Dietary Fibre 2.5 g; Cholesterol
222 mg; 2165 kJ (515 Cal)

Garlic prawns (top), and
Veal Parmigiana

MINESTRONE

Prep time: 35 minutes
Cooking time: 1 hour
    45 minutes
Serves 6

2 tablespoons olive oil
100 g pancetta or bacon,
    cut into short, thin strips
1 large onion, finely chopped
2 cloves garlic, crushed
1 celery stick, halved
    lengthwise and cut into
    1 cm slices
1 carrot, halved lengthwise
    and cut into 1 cm slices
1 large potato, peeled and
    cut into 1 cm cubes
1 tablespoon tomato paste
400 g can diced Italian
    tomatoes
8 fresh basil leaves, torn
2 litres chicken stock
100 g pumpkin, peeled and
    cut into 1 cm cubes
400 g can borlotti beans,
    rinsed and drained
2 zucchini, halved lengthwise
    and cut into 5 mm pieces
50 g silverbeet leaves,
    shredded
80 g green beans, cut into
    4 cm lengths
50 g cabbage, finely
    shredded
75 g ditalini

Pesto

2 cups (100 g) fresh basil
    leaves
35 g pine nuts, toasted
2 cloves garlic, crushed
1/2 cup (125 ml) olive oil
70 g grated Parmesan

Minestrone

1 Heat the oil in a large saucepan. Add the pancetta or bacon, onion and garlic and cook over low heat, stirring occasionally, for 10 minutes, or until the onion is soft and golden.
2 Add the celery, carrot and potato to the pan, cook for 5 minutes, then stir in the tomato paste, tomatoes and torn basil leaves. Season with plenty of freshly ground black pepper. Add the chicken stock and slowly bring to the boil over medium heat. Cover, reduce the heat to low and simmer, stirring occasionally, for 1 hour. Don't worry if the potato starts to break up, it will help to thicken the soup. Add the pumpkin and borlotti beans, then simmer, uncovered, for 15 minutes. Add the zucchini, silverbeet, green beans, cabbage and ditalini, and simmer for 10 minutes, or until the pasta is *al dente*. Season with salt and pepper.
3 Meanwhile, to make the pesto, place the basil, pine nuts and garlic in a food processor and, with the motor running, gradually add the olive oil until the mixture forms a paste. Stir in the Parmesan and season to taste. Serve the soup topped with a dollop of pesto, and accompanied by fresh, crusty bread.

Nutrition per serve: Fat 37.5 g, Protein 19 g; Carbohydrate 27 g; Dietary Fibre 6 g; Cholesterol 20.5 mg; 2145 kJ (510 Cal)

Notes: Traditionally minestrone is made using dried borlotti or cannellini beans, which will have a better flavour than the canned variety. If you have time, try substituting 125 g dried beans for the canned beans. Soak them in water overnight, then drain and rinse. Add the soaked beans to the soup with the tomatoes and fresh basil.

There are many different variations on this popular Mediterranean soup. While pancetta offers a richness of flavour, it can be omitted, and vegetable stock can be used instead of chicken to make a vegetarian version. Don't be constrained by the vegetables listed, almost anything fresh and seasonal is a great addition. Traditionally this soup is made in large quantities as the flavours develop overnight and leftovers are often even better than the freshly made soup.

Prep time: ...minutes +
...frigeration
Cooking time: 2 hours
   25 minutes
Serves 4–6

1.5 kg chicken
1 onion
2 large leeks, halved
   lengthwise and well
   washed
3 large celery sticks
5 black peppercorns
1 bay leaf
2 large carrots, peeled and
   diced
1 large swede, peeled and
   diced
2 large tomatoes, peeled,
   seeded and finely chopped
3/4 cup (165 g) barley
1 tablespoon tomato paste
2 tablespoons finely
   chopped fresh flat-leaf
   parsley

1 Place the chicken,
onion, 1 leek, 1 stick
of celery, halved, the
peppercorns and bay leaf
in a large saucepan and
add enough water to
cover. Bring to the boil,
then reduce the heat and
simmer for 1 1/2 hours,
skimming any impurities
that rise to the surface.
Strain the stock through
a fine sieve and return
to the cleaned saucepan.
Discard the onion, leek,
celery, peppercorns and
bay leaf, and set the
chicken aside. When it

is cool enough to handle,
discard the fat and bones,
then shred the flesh,
cover and chill.
2 Allow the stock to
cool, then refrigerate
overnight. Skim the fat
from the surface, place
the stock in a large
saucepan and bring
to the boil. Dice the
remaining celery and
leek, and add to the soup
with the carrot, swede,
tomato, barley and
tomato paste. Simmer
for 45–50 minutes, or
until the vegetables are
cooked and the barley is
tender. Stir in the parsley
and shredded chicken.
Simmer until warmed
through and season.

Nutrition per serve (6): Fat 8 g;
Protein 27 g; Carbohydrate 24 g;
Dietary Fibre 8; Cholesterol
87 mg; 1145 kJ (275 Cal)

CLASSIC OMELETTE
Prep time: 2 minutes
Cooking time: 2 minutes
Serves 1

3 eggs
10 g butter

1 Break the eggs into
a small bowl. Add
2 tablespoons water,
season with salt and
freshly ground black
pepper, and beat
together well. Heat the
butter in a small frying

pan or omelette pan
over high heat. When
the butter is foaming,
reduce the heat to
medium, and add the
egg mixture all at once.
Tilt the pan to cover the
base with the egg and
leave for a few seconds.
Using a spatula or egg
flip, draw the sides of the
omelette into the centre
and let any extra liquid
egg run to the edges.
2 If you are adding a
filling to the omelette,
sprinkle it over the egg.
As soon as the egg is
almost set, use an egg
slide to fold the omelette
in half in the pan. It
should still be soft inside.
Slide it onto a warm
serving plate and serve
immediately.

Nutrition per serve: Fat 24.5 g;
Protein 21 g; Carbohydrate 1 g;
Dietary Fibre 0 g; Cholesterol
633 mg; 1275 kJ (305 Cal)

Fillings

Sprinkle the omelette with 1/3 cup
(15 g) roughly torn rocket and
50 g crumbled goat's cheese.

Saute 2/3 cup (60 g) finely sliced
button mushrooms with 20 g
butter, add 1 tablespoon finely
chopped fresh basil, and scatter
over the omelette.

Sprinkle with 50 g cooked crab
meat and 20 g bean sprouts.
Drizzle with 2 teaspoons oyster
sauce before serving.

Chicken and vegetable
soup (top), and Classic
omelette with rocket
and goat's cheese

CHILLI CON CARNE

Prep time: 10 minutes
Cooking time: 1 hour
    10 minutes
Serves 4

2 teaspoons ground cumin
1/2 teaspoon ground allspice
1–2 teaspoons chilli powder
1 teaspoon paprika
1 tablespoon vegetable oil
1 large onion, finely chopped
2 cloves garlic, crushed
2 small fresh red chillies,
    seeded and finely chopped
500 g lean beef mince
400 g can whole tomatoes
2 tablespoons tomato paste
425 g can red kidney beans,
    drained and rinsed
1 cup (250 ml) beef stock
1 tablespoon chopped fresh
    oregano
1 teaspoon sugar

1 Heat a small frying pan over medium heat and dry-fry the cumin, allspice, chilli and paprika for 1 minute, or until they are fragrant. Remove from the pan.
2 Heat the oil in a large saucepan over medium heat and cook the onion for 2–3 minutes, or until soft. Add the garlic and fresh chilli, and cook for 1 minute. Add the mince and cook over high heat for 4–5 minutes, or until browned, breaking up any lumps with a fork.

Chilli con carne (top), and
Tuna Niçoise

3 Add the tomatoes, tomato paste, kidney beans, stock, oregano, sugar and spices. Reduce the heat and simmer, stirring occasionally and gently breaking up the tomatoes, for 1 hour or until reduced and thickened. Season with salt and black pepper. Delicious served with tortillas and guacamole (see recipe on page 57).

Nutrition per serve: Fat 14.5 g; Protein 33 g; Carbohydrate 19 g; Dietary Fibre 7.5 g; Cholesterol 63.5 mg; 1400 kJ (335 Cal)

TUNA NICOISE

Prep time: 15 minutes
Cooking time: 15 minutes
Serves 4

425 g can tuna in brine
200 g green beans, trimmed
10 small chat potatoes
3 eggs
1/3 cup (80 ml) olive oil
2 teaspoons white wine
    vinegar
2 teaspoons lemon juice
1–2 mignonette lettuces,
    washed
4 small tomatoes, quartered
20 black olives
4 anchovy fillets, rinsed and
    halved lengthwise (optional)

1 Drain the tuna and place in a bowl. Break up any large chunks with a fork, cover and chill until needed.

2 Bring a saucepan of water to the boil and cook the green beans for 1 minute, then remove and rinse under cold water, retaining the cooking water. Return the cooking water to the boil and add the chat potatoes. Boil for 10 minutes or until tender. Rinse under cold water, then cut the potatoes in half. Meanwhile, fill a saucepan with cold water. Add the eggs, bring to the boil over high heat and boil for 10 minutes. Drain, and when cool enough to handle, peel and cut into quarters.
3 Place the oil, vinegar and lemon juice in a jar with a screwtop lid. Season with salt and black pepper, and shake well to combine. Place the beans and potatoes in a bowl with the tuna and 2 tablespoons of the dressing, and gently toss to combine. Place the mignonette leaves on a serving platter and pile the tuna mixture on top. Arrange the tomato and egg quarters around the salad, top with olives and anchovies, and drizzle with the remaining dressing.

Nutrition per serve: Fat 23.5 g; Protein 21 g; Carbohydrate 30 g; Dietary Fibre 6 g; Cholesterol 186 mg; 1750 kJ (420 Cal)

QUICHE LORRAINE

Prep time: 25 minutes +
   50 minutes refrigeration
Cooking time: 1 hour
Serves 4–6

1 1/2 cups (185 g) plain flour
100 g butter, chilled and
   chopped
1–2 tablespoons iced water
1 tablespoon oil
4 rashers bacon, chopped
1 onion, chopped
50 g Cheddar, grated
   (see Note)
3 eggs
1/4 cup (60 ml) milk
1 cup (250 ml) cream

1 Sift the flour into a large bowl and add the butter. Rub the butter into the flour with your fingertips until the mixture resembles fine breadcrumbs. Add enough iced water to form a soft dough, using a flat-bladed knife to mix it in with a cutting, rather than a stirring action. Turn the dough out onto a lightly floured surface and gather it together into a smooth ball. Do not knead or the pastry will become tough. Cover with plastic wrap and chill for 30 minutes.

2 Preheat the oven to moderately hot 200°C (400°F/Gas 6). Lightly grease a 22 cm deep, fluted flan tin. Unwrap the dough and roll it out between two large sheets of baking paper to a 30 cm diameter circle. Remove the top sheet of baking paper and invert the pastry into the prepared tin. Use a small ball of dough to press the pastry into the tin, allowing any excess to hang over the edge. Run the rolling pin over the tin, cutting off the excess pastry, and chill the shell for 20 minutes. Line the pastry with a piece of lightly crumpled baking paper that is large enough to cover the base and side, and fill with baking beads or uncooked rice. Bake for 15 minutes, then remove the paper and beads, and return the pastry to the oven for 10 minutes, or until the base is dry and lightly browned, with no greasy patches. Leave to cool.

3 Reduce the oven temperature to moderate 180°C (350°F/Gas 4) and place a baking tray in the oven to heat. Heat the oil in a frying pan over medium heat and cook the bacon and onion for 5 minutes, or until just starting to brown. Remove from the heat and drain on crumpled paper towels. Place the pastry shell on the preheated tray, then sprinkle the bacon, onion and Cheddar evenly over the base. Whisk the eggs, milk and cream together in a large bowl and season with salt and freshly ground black pepper. Pour the egg mixture into the pastry case over the bacon, onion and cheese, and bake for 20–25 minutes or until just set. Serve warm with a fresh tossed green salad.

Nutrition per serve (6): Fat 44 g; Protein 17 g; Carbohydrate 28 g; Dietary Fibre 1.5 g; Cholesterol 228 mg; 2375 kJ (570 Cal)

Note: Gruyère, which has a much stronger flavour than Cheddar, is commonly used in a quiche Lorraine. You may wish to substitute Gruyère for some or all of the Cheddar in this recipe. This is a dish from Nancy, a town in the region of Lorraine, in France. It was originally made without cheese and served as part of the May day festivities to celebrate the start of spring.

Quiche Lorraine

PASTA CARBONARA

Prep time: 10 minutes
Cooking time: 15 minutes
Serves 4

300 g penne rigate
1 tablespoon extra virgin olive oil
200 g piece pancetta, cut into short, thin strips
200 ml cream
1 clove garlic, crushed
6 egg yolks
1 1/2 cups (150 g) grated reggiano Parmesan
1 tablespoon finely chopped fresh flat-leaf parsley

1 Cook the penne in a large saucepan of rapidly boiling water until *al dente*. Drain well and return to the pan.
2 Meanwhile, heat the oil in a large frying pan over medium–high heat and cook the pancetta for 3–4 minutes, or until crisp. Remove and drain on paper towels.
3 Beat the cream, garlic and egg yolks together in a bowl, and season with salt and pepper. Stir in half the Parmesan. Stir the pancetta into the hot pasta, allowing the oil from the pancetta to coat the pasta. Add the egg mixture immediately, and stir to combine — the heat from the pasta will cook the eggs. Stir in

Pasta carbonara (top), and Beef satay

the chopped parsley. Serve sprinkled with the remaining Parmesan and some freshly cracked black pepper.

Nutrition per serve: Fat 51 g; Protein 35 g; Carbohydrate 53 g; Dietary Fibre 2.5 g; Cholesterol 396.5 mg; 3380 kJ (805 Cal)

BEEF SATAY

Prep time: 25 minutes +
  3 hours marinating
Cooking time: 25 minutes
Serves 4

700 g rump steak, cut into 2.5 cm cubes
2 small cloves garlic, crushed
3 teaspoons grated fresh ginger
1 tablespoon fish sauce
2 small fresh red chillies, seeded and julienned

Satay sauce
1 tablespoon peanut oil
8 red Asian shallots, finely chopped
8 cloves garlic, crushed
4 small fresh red chillies, finely chopped
1 tablespoon finely chopped fresh ginger
1 cup (250 g) crunchy peanut butter
400 ml coconut milk
1 tablespoon soy sauce
1/3 cup (60 g) grated palm sugar
3 tablespoons fish sauce
1 fresh kaffir lime leaf
4 tablespoons lime juice

1 C...
with t...
and fish
marinate, ...
the refrigera...
least 3 hours. ...
soak 8 wooden
in cold water for
2 To make the satay sauce, heat the peanut oil in a saucepan over medium heat. Cook the shallots, garlic, chilli and ginger, stirring occasionally, for 5 minutes, or until the shallots are golden. Reduce the heat to low and add the peanut butter, coconut milk, soy sauce, palm sugar, fish sauce, lime leaf and lime juice. Simmer for 10 minutes, or until thickened, then remove the lime leaf.
3 Thread the beef onto the skewers and cook on a barbecue or chargrill pan over high heat for 6–8 minutes, or until cooked though, turning halfway. Top with the satay sauce and garnish with the julienned chilli. Serve with rice.

Nutrition per serve: Fat 73 g; Protein 64 g; Carbohydrate 29 g; Dietary Fibre 12.5 g; Cholesterol 112 mg; 4275 kJ (1020 Cal)

. 20 minutes +
..nutes marinating
..ing time: 20 minutes
..rves 4

1 tablespoon cornflour
2 teaspoons finely chopped
  fresh ginger
2 cloves garlic, crushed
1 small fresh red chilli, finely
  chopped
1 teaspoon sesame oil
1/4 cup (60 ml) light soy
  sauce
500 g chicken breast fillet,
  thinly sliced
1 tablespoon peanut oil
1 onion, halved and thinly
  sliced
115 g baby corn, halved on
  the diagonal
425 g baby bok choy,
  trimmed and quartered
  lengthwise
2 tablespoons oyster sauce
1/4 cup (60 ml) chicken stock

1 Combine half the
cornflour with the
ginger, crushed garlic,
chilli, sesame oil and
2 tablespoons soy sauce
in a large bowl. Add the
chicken, toss until well
coated and marinate for
10 minutes.
2 Heat a wok over high
heat, add the peanut oil
and swirl to coat. Stir-fry
the onion for 2 minutes,
or until soft and golden.
Add the chicken in two
batches and stir-fry for

5 minutes, or until almost
cooked through. Add the
baby corn and stir-fry for
a further 2 minutes, then
add the bok choy and
cook for 2 minutes, or
until wilted.
3 Mix the remaining
soy sauce and cornflour
with the oyster sauce
and chicken stock in
a small bowl, add to
the wok and stir-fry for
1–2 minutes, or until the
sauce has thickened to
coating consistency and
the chicken is cooked.
Serve immediately with
steamed rice or noodles.

Nutrition per serve: Fat 13.5 g;
Protein 31 g; Carbohydrate 13 g;
Dietary Fibre 3.5 g; Cholesterol
82.5 mg; 1245 kJ (295 Cal)

PEA AND HAM SOUP

Prep time: 20 minutes +
  6 hours soaking
Cooking time: 2 hours
  10 minutes
Serves 6–8

500 g yellow or green split
  peas
1 1/2 tablespoons olive oil
2 onions, chopped
1 carrot, diced
3 celery sticks, finely chopped
1 kg ham bones or a smoked
  ham hock, chopped
  (see Notes)
1 bay leaf
2 sprigs fresh thyme
lemon juice, to taste (optional)

1 Place the peas in a
large bowl, cover with
cold water and soak for
6 hours. Drain well.
2 Heat the oil in a large
saucepan, add the onion,
carrot and celery, and
cook over low heat for
6–7 minutes, or until
the vegetables are soft
but not brown.
3 Add the split peas,
ham bones, bay leaf,
thyme and 2.5 litres
of cold water, and bring
to the boil. Reduce the
heat and simmer, stirring
occasionally, for 2 hours,
or until the peas are
tender, removing any
scum that rises to the
surface. Discard the
bay leaf and thyme.
4 Remove the ham
bones from the soup,
cool slightly, then
remove the meat from
the bones and discard
the bones. Return the
ham to the soup and
reheat. Season to taste
with pepper and lemon
juice, if desired.

Nutrition per serve (8): Fat 7.5 g;
Protein 19 g; Carbohydrate 31 g;
Dietary Fibre 7 g; Cholesterol
13 mg; 1110 kJ (265 Cal)

Notes: Ask your butcher to chop
the ham bones for you.

For a smoother texture, the soup
can be cooled and processed
once the ham bones have been
removed. Return the meat to the
puréed soup.

Easy chicken stir-fry (top),
and Pea and ham soup

LASAGNE

Prep time: 35 minutes +
30 minutes standing
Cooking time: 3 hours
30 minutes
Serves 6

30 g butter
1 onion, finely chopped
2 cloves garlic, crushed
1 celery stick, finely chopped
1 carrot, finely chopped
50 g sliced pancetta, finely
chopped
500 g beef mince
1 tablespoon chopped
fresh oregano
1 cup (250 ml) red wine
2 cups (500 ml) beef stock
2 tablespoons tomato paste
2 x 400 g cans crushed
tomatoes

350 g fresh lasagne sheets
1/2 cup (75 g) grated
mozzarella
2 tablespoons grated
Parmesan

Bèchamel sauce
600 ml milk
1/2 onion, chopped
2 cloves garlic, crushed
1 bay leaf
30 g butter
1/2 cup (60 g) plain flour
150 ml cream
1/2 teaspoon ground nutmeg
2 tablespoons grated
Parmesan

1 Melt the butter in a large saucepan, add the onion and cook over medium heat for 2–3 minutes, or until it starts to soften. Add the garlic, celery and carrot, and cook, stirring, over low heat for 5 minutes. Increase the heat to high, add the pancetta, beef and oregano, and cook for 4–5 minutes, or until the meat is browned. Use a fork to break up any lumps. Stir in the red wine and simmer for 2–3 minutes, or until it is absorbed. Add the stock, tomato paste and the crushed tomatoes, then season well with salt and freshly cracked black pepper. Reduce the heat to low, cover with a lid and simmer for 1 hour 30 minutes, stirring occasionally to prevent it from catching on the bottom of the pan. Remove the lid and simmer for another hour, stirring occasionally.

2 Meanwhile, to make the bèchamel sauce, place the milk in a large saucepan with the onion, garlic and bay leaf, and bring up to simmering point. Turn off the heat and leave to infuse for 30 minutes, then strain. Melt the butter in a saucepan over medium heat, stir in the flour and cook for 1 minute, or until it is foaming. Remove from the heat and gradually stir in the infused milk. Return the pan to the heat and stir constantly until the sauce boils and thickens. Reduce the heat to low and stir in the cream. Simmer for 5 minutes, stirring occasionally. Remove from the heat and season with salt and black pepper. Stir in the ground nutmeg and grated Parmesan. Pour the sauce into a clean bowl and cover with plastic wrap, resting it on the surface of the sauce to prevent a skin forming. Allow to cool.

3 Preheat the oven to moderate 180°C (350°F/ Gas 4) and grease a 2 litre ovenproof dish. Spread half of the meat sauce on the bottom of the dish and cover with a layer of pasta sheets, cutting to fit if necessary. Spread with half of the bèchamel sauce and half of the grated mozzarella. Repeat to give a second layer, and scatter the Parmesan over the top. Bake for 40 minutes, or until bubbling and golden. Allow the lasagne to rest for 10 minutes before cutting. Serve with a green salad if desired.

Nutrition per serve: Fat 34.5 g;
Protein 33 g; Carbohydrate 36 g;
Dietary Fibre 4.5 g; Cholesterol
131.5 mg; 2550 kJ (610 Cal)

Note: If the top of the lasagne
browns too quickly, cover it
loosely with foil.

Lasagne

[CHICK]EN AND [MUSH]ROOM RISOTTO

Prep time: 15 minutes
Cooking time: 45 minutes
Serves 4

1.25 litres vegetable or
    chicken stock
2 tablespoons olive oil
300 g chicken breast fillets,
    cut into 1.5 cm wide strips
250 g small button
    mushrooms, halved
pinch nutmeg
2 cloves garlic, crushed
20 g butter
1 small onion, finely chopped
375 g arborio rice
2/3 cup (170 ml) dry white
    wine
3 tablespoons sour cream
45 g freshly grated
    Parmesan
3 tablespoons finely
    chopped fresh flat-leaf
    parsley

1 Bring the stock to the boil over high heat, reduce the heat and keep at a simmer. Heat the oil in a large saucepan. Cook the chicken pieces over high heat for 3–4 minutes, or until golden brown. Add the mushrooms and cook for 1–2 minutes more, or until starting to brown. Stir in the nutmeg and garlic, and season with salt and freshly ground black pepper. Cook for 30 seconds then remove from the pan.

2 Melt the butter in the same pan and cook the onion over low heat for 5–6 minutes. Add the rice, stir to coat, then stir in the wine. Once the wine is absorbed, reduce the heat and add 1/2 cup (125 ml) of the stock, stirring constantly over medium heat until all the liquid is absorbed. Continue adding more liquid, 1/2 cup (125 ml) at a time, until all the stock has been used and the rice is creamy. This will take about 20–25 minutes. Stir in the mushrooms and the chicken with the last of the chicken stock.

3 Remove the pan from the heat and stir in the sour cream, Parmesan and parsley. Season before serving.

Nutrition per serve: Fat 29 g;
Protein 33 g; Carbohydrate 79 g;
Dietary Fibre 3 g; Cholesterol
92 mg; 3075 kJ (735 Cal)

VEAL MARSALA

Prep time: 10 minutes
Cooking time: 10 minutes
Serves 4

4 pieces (500 g) veal schnitzel
plain flour, for dusting
45 g butter
1 tablespoon oil
2/3 cup (185 ml) dry Marsala
3 teaspoons cream
30 g butter, chopped, extra

1 Using a meat mallet or the heel of your hand, flatten the schitzel pieces to 5 mm thick. Season the flour well and dust the veal to coat, shaking off any excess. Heat the butter and oil in a large frying pan and cook the veal over medium–high heat for 1–2 minutes on each side, or until almost cooked through. Remove and keep warm.

2 Add the Marsala to the pan and bring to the boil, scraping the base of the pan to loosen any sediment. Reduce the heat and simmer for 1–2 minutes, or until slightly reduced. Add the cream and simmer for 2 minutes more, then whisk in the extra butter until the sauce thickens slightly. Return the veal to the pan and simmer for 1 minute, or until the meat is warmed through. Serve immediately. Delicious with a creamy garlic mash and a tossed green salad.

Nutrition per serve: Fat 24.5 g;
Protein 28 g; Carbohydrate 8 g;
Dietary Fibre 0 g; Cholesterol
154.5 mg; 1690 kJ (405 Cal)

Note: Purchase veal that is very
pale in colour and free of sinew.
The pale colour indicates young,
tender meat, and sinew will
make the meat tough.

Chicken and
mushroom risotto (top),
and Veal Marsala

MEATLOAF

Prep time: 20 minutes +
    10 minutes standing
Cooking time: 1 hour
Serves 6–8

2 tablespoons olive oil
2 large onions, finely
    chopped
3 cloves garlic, crushed
1 tablespoon tomato paste
2 cups (160 g) fresh
    breadcrumbs
1/4 cup (60 ml) red wine
500 g beef mince
250 g veal mince
250 g pork mince
1/2 cup (15 g) finely chopped
    fresh flat-leaf parsley
2 tablespoons chopped
    fresh chives
1 teaspoon chopped fresh
    thyme
2 teaspoons chopped fresh
    sage
1 teaspoon ground nutmeg
2 tablespoons
    Worcestershire sauce
2 tablespoons Dijon mustard
2 eggs, lightly beaten

Barbecue sauce
2 teaspoons oil
1 small onion, finely chopped
1 tablespoon malt vinegar
1 tablespoon soft brown
    sugar
1/3 cup (80 ml) tomato sauce
1 tablespoon Worcestershire
    sauce

1 Preheat the oven to
moderate 180°C (350°F/
Gas 4). Heat half of the

Meatloaf

olive oil in a frying pan
over medium heat, add
the onion and cook for
8–10 minutes, or until
soft and golden. Stir
in the garlic and tomato
paste, and continue
cooking for 5 minutes.
Remove from the heat
and allow to cool.
2 Place the breadcrumbs
in a small bowl and pour
the wine over them. Stir
to combine, and leave
to soak. Combine the
beef, veal and pork
mince, parsley, chives,
thyme, sage, nutmeg,
Worcestershire sauce,
Dijon mustard, eggs
and onion mixture in
a large bowl. Add the
breadcrumb mixture,
season, and mix until
well combined. Place
in a 20 x 9 x 6 cm loaf
tin, pressing the loaf
to eliminate any air
pockets. Brush the
top of the loaf with
the remaining oil.
3 Place the loaf tin in
a deep ovenproof dish
and pour enough hot
water into the dish to
come halfway up the
sides of the tin. Bake
for 40–45 minutes, or
until cooked through
when tested with a
skewer. The juices
should run clear and
the loaf should be firm
to the touch. Remove
from the oven and leave
for 10 minutes.
4 Meanwhile, to make
the barbecue sauce, heat

the oil in a saucepan
over medium heat. Add
the chopped onion and
cook for 3 minutes,
or until soft, stirring
occasionally. Add the
malt vinegar, brown
sugar, tomato sauce
and Worcestershire
sauce, and bring to
the boil. Reduce the
heat and simmer for
3 minutes. Keep warm
until ready to serve.
5 Remove the meatloaf
from the tin and cut into
2 cm slices. Serve with
the barbecue sauce and
a green salad if desired.

Nutrition per serve (8): Fat 17 g;
Protein 31 g; Carbohydrate 20 g;
Dietary Fibre 2.5 g; Cholesterol
127 mg; 1480 kJ (355 Cal)

Note: The barbecue sauce will
keep well in the refrigerator for
up to 1 week. The meatloaf will
keep for up to 2 days, covered,
in the refrigerator. Leftover
meatloaf can be eaten hot or
cold, and is great in sandwiches.

SAUSAGES WITH CREAMY MASH AND ONION GRAVY

Prep time: 20 minutes
Cooking time: 45 minutes
Serves 4

1 tablespoon olive oil
8 thick sausages (pork or
    Bratwurst)

Onion gravy
40 g butter
3 onions, thinly sliced
2 cloves garlic, crushed
1 tablespoon plain flour
2 cups (500 ml) beef stock
1/2 cup (125 ml) dry white
    wine
2 teaspoons Dijon mustard
3 teaspoons soft brown
    sugar
1 teaspoon chopped fresh
    thyme

Creamy mash
4 large potatoes, peeled
    (pontiac, desiree or
    sebago)
1/2 cup (125 ml) milk
30 g butter, cut into cubes

1 Heat the oil in a large frying pan. Cook the sausages over medium–high heat for 5 minutes, or until browned on all sides. Remove to a plate and keep warm.
2 To make the onion gravy, melt the butter in the same frying pan, add the onion and cook over low heat for 15 minutes, or until soft and golden. Add the garlic and cook for 30 seconds. Stir in the flour and cook over low heat for 1 minute to brown. Remove the pan from the heat and gradually add the stock and wine. Return to the heat and bring to the boil. Stir in the mustard, sugar and thyme, then reduce the heat and simmer gently, stirring occasionally, for 10 minutes, or until thickened. Season to taste with pepper. Add the sausages to the gravy and simmer, stirring, for 8–10 minutes, or until cooked through.
3 Meanwhile, cut the potatoes into small, even chunks and boil for 10 minutes, or until tender, then drain well. Return the potato to the saucepan, stirring for 20 seconds over low heat to remove any excess moisture. Heat the milk in a small saucepan to just simmering, then add the hot milk to the potato and mash until lump-free. Add the butter and stir in until the potato is smooth and creamy. Season well. Serve the sausages and gravy over the mashed potato with a salad or steamed vegetables.

Nutrition per serve: Fat 52 g; Protein 25 g; Carbohydrate 36 g; Dietary Fibre 5.5 g; Cholesterol 141.5 mg; 3040 kJ (725 Cal)

Note: As an alternative to adding the butter to the mash, replace with 1 1/2 tablespoons extra virgin olive oil and 1 tablespoon finely chopped fresh flat-leaf parsley.

PASTA WITH PESTO

Prep time: 15 minutes
Cooking time: 15 minutes
Serves 4

500 g spaghetti
3 cups (150 g) fresh basil
    leaves
1/3 cup (50 g) pine nuts,
    lightly toasted
3 cloves garlic, peeled
3/4 cup (185 ml) olive oil
1 cup (100 g) grated
    Parmesan

1 Cook the spaghetti in a saucepan of rapidly boiling water until *al dente*. Drain well and return to the saucepan.
2 Meanwhile, place the basil, pine nuts and garlic in a food processor and, with the motor running, gradually pour in the oil to form a paste. Stir in the grated Parmesan and season. Toss the pesto through the hot pasta until well combined. Serve immediately.

Nutrition per serve: Fat 58 g; Protein 25 g; Carbohydrate 87 g; Dietary Fibre 6 g; Cholesterol 20 mg; 4035 kJ (965 Cal)

Sausages with creamy mash and onion gravy (top), and Pasta with pesto

PUMPKIN SOUP

Prep time: 15 minutes
Cooking time: 35 minutes
Serves 4

2 kg butternut pumpkin
40 g butter
2 onions, chopped
1/2 teaspoon cumin seeds
1 litre chicken stock
1 bay leaf
1/3 cup (80 ml) cream
pinch nutmeg

1 Peel the pumpkin and chop into small chunks. Melt the butter in a large saucepan, add the onion and cook over low heat for 5–7 minutes, or until soft. Add the cumin seeds and cook for 1 minute, then add the pumpkin pieces, stock and bay leaf. Increase the heat to high and bring to the boil, then reduce the heat and simmer for 20 minutes, or until the pumpkin is soft. Remove the bay leaf, and allow the soup to cool slightly.
2 Blend the soup in batches until smooth. Return to the cleaned saucepan and stir in the cream and nutmeg. Simmer gently until warmed through and season with salt and freshly ground black pepper before serving.

Pumpkin soup (top), and Osso buco with gremolata

Nutrition per serve: Fat 19.5 g; Protein 11 g; Carbohydrate 25 g; Dietary Fibre 4.5 g; Cholesterol 54 mg; 1305 kJ (310 Cal)

OSSO BUCO WITH GREMOLATA

Prep time: 20 minutes
Cooking time: 3 hours
Serves 4

8 pieces (about 1.4 kg) veal
  shanks, cut osso buco style
1/2 cup (60 g) plain flour,
  seasoned
20 g butter
3 tablespoons vegetable oil
1 carrot, finely chopped
1 large onion, finely chopped
1/2 celery stick, finely
  chopped
1 clove garlic, crushed
2/3 cup (170 ml) dry white
  wine
3 cups (750 ml) chicken
  stock
400 g can diced tomatoes
1 bouquet garni (see Note)

Gremolata
1 tablespoon grated lemon
  rind
2/3 cup (20 g) finely chopped
  fresh flat-leaf parsley
2 cloves garlic, finely
  chopped

1 Coat the pieces of veal in flour, shaking off any excess. Heat the butter and 2 tablespoons of the oil in a flameproof casserole dish or large saucepan. Gently cook the veal, in two batches, for 5 minutes on each side, or until brown, turning once. Remove.
2 Add the remaining oil to the dish and stir in the carrot, onion, celery and garlic. Cook, stirring, over low heat, for about 5–6 minutes, or until soft. Do not allow the mixture to brown. Add the wine and cook over high heat for 1–2 minutes, then add the stock, tomato and bouquet garni. Season to taste.
3 Return the veal to the pan, arranging it in a single layer. Cover, reduce the heat and simmer for 2 hours 30 minutes, or until the meat is tender and falling off the bone, and the sauce has reduced slightly. If the sauce seems too thin, remove the shanks and boil over high heat for 10 minutes, or until it is reduced. Remove and discard the bouquet garni.
4 Combine the gremolata ingredients, and sprinkle over the osso buco just before serving. Delicious served with soft polenta.

Nutrition per serve: Fat 27.5 g; Protein 66 g; Carbohydrate 21 g; Dietary Fibre 3.5 g; Cholesterol 246 mg; 2685 kJ (640 Cal)

Note: To make a bouquet garni, wrap the green part of a leek around 1 sprig parsley, 1 sprig oregano and 2 bay leaves, and tie with string.

PASTA WITH FRESH TOMATO AND BASIL SAUCE

Prep time: 15 minutes
Cooking time: 15 minutes
Serves 4

500 g penne rigate
1/3 cup (80 ml) extra virgin
olive oil
4 cloves garlic, crushed
4 anchovy fillets, finely
chopped
2 small fresh red chillies,
seeded and finely chopped
6 large, vine-ripened
tomatoes, peeled, seeded
and diced
1/3 cup (80 ml) white wine
1 tablespoon tomato paste
2 teaspoons sugar
2 tablespoons finely
chopped fresh flat-leaf
parsley
3 tablespoons shredded
fresh basil

1 Cook the pasta in a saucepan of boiling water until *al dente*. Drain well.
2 Meanwhile heat the oil in a frying pan, and cook the garlic for 30 seconds. Stir in the anchovy and chilli, and cook for a further 30 seconds. Add the tomato, and cook for 2 minutes over high heat. Add the wine, tomato paste and sugar, and simmer, covered, for 10 minutes, or until thickened.
3 Toss the tomato sauce through the pasta with the herbs. Season, and serve with freshly grated Parmesan, if desired.

Nutrition per serve: Fat 19.5 g;
Protein 19 g; Carbohydrate 94 g;
Dietary Fibre 8.5 g; Cholesterol
3 mg; 2700 kJ (645 Cal)

COTTAGE PIE

Prep time: 20 minutes
Cooking time: 1 hour
20 minutes
Serves 6

900 g potatoes, peeled and
cut into 3 cm pieces
45 g butter
2–3 tablespoons milk
2 tablespoons oil
2 onions, finely chopped
1 clove garlic, crushed
1 kg beef mince
1/4 cup (30 g) plain flour
1 1/2 cups (375 ml) beef
stock
1/4 cup (60 g) tomato paste
3 teaspoons Worcestershire
sauce
1/4 teaspoon mustard
powder
2 tablespoons chopped
fresh flat-leaf parsley

1 Preheat the oven to moderate 180°C (350°F/ Gas 4) and grease a 2 litre ovenproof dish. Boil the potatoes for 10 minutes, or until tender, then drain well. Return to the saucepan, add the butter and mash until smooth and free of lumps. Add enough milk to give a firm consistency. Season.
2 Heat the oil in a frying pan over medium heat, and cook the onion and garlic for 5 minutes, or until soft. Add the beef and cook over high heat for 8–10 minutes, or until the meat is browned and most of the liquid has evaporated. Break up any lumps with a fork. Add the flour and cook, stirring, for 2 minutes, or until well combined.
3 Slowly add the stock and stir for 3–4 minutes, or until it has thickened. Remove from the heat and stir in the tomato paste, Worcestershire sauce, mustard and parsley. Season with salt and freshly ground pepper, and pour into the prepared dish.
4 Spread the mash over the meat mixture. Use a fork to decorate the top with peaks and swirls, and bake for 50 minutes, or until the potato is golden. Rest the pie for 5 minutes before serving.

Nutrition per serve: Fat 24.5 g;
Protein 40 g; Carbohydrate 29 g;
Dietary Fibre 3.5 g; Cholesterol
105 mg; 2065 kJ (495 Cal)

Pasta with fresh tomato
and basil sauce (top),
and Cottage pie

GREEN CHICKEN CURRY

Prep time: 20 minutes
Cooking time: 40 minutes
Serves 4

Curry paste
1 tablespoon shrimp paste
1/2 teaspoon cumin seeds, toasted
1 teaspoon coriander seeds, toasted
1/4 teaspoon white peppercorns
5 fresh coriander roots
3 tablespoons chopped fresh galangal
10 fresh long green chillies, chopped
1 stem lemon grass (white part only), roughly chopped
6 red Asian shallots, peeled
3 cloves garlic, peeled
1 teaspoon grated kaffir lime rind or lime rind
2 tablespoons peanut oil

2 tablespoons peanut oil
3 slender eggplants, cut into 5 mm slices
140 g can thick coconut cream
400 ml can coconut milk
500 g chicken breast fillet, thinly sliced
5 kaffir lime leaves, shredded
1–1 1/2 tablespoons fish sauce
1 tablespoon shaved palm sugar
1 tablespoon lime juice
1/4 cup (15 g) fresh Thai basil leaves, plus extra, to garnish

Green chicken curry

1 Preheat the oven to moderate 180°C (350°F/ Gas 4). Wrap the shrimp paste in foil, place in an ovenproof dish and bake for 5–10 minutes or until fragrant. Meanwhile, place the cumin seeds, coriander seeds and peppercorns in a spice grinder or mortar and pestle and grind to a fine powder. Place the spice powder in a food processor with the coriander roots, galangal, chilli, lemon grass, Asian shallots, garlic, kaffir lime rind, shrimp paste, peanut oil and 1/4 teaspoon salt, and process until smooth.

2 Heat a wok over high heat, add the peanut oil and swirl to coat the side of the wok. Add the eggplant and stir-fry for 2 minutes, or until browned, then remove from the wok.

3 Add the coconut cream to the wok and cook over medium–high heat for 8–10 minutes, or until the cream separates. Add 1–1 1/2 tablespoons of the curry paste and continue stirring for 1–2 minutes, or until fragrant. Slowly pour in the coconut milk, stirring constantly, then bring to a gentle simmer and cook for 5 minutes, or until a green oil separates and comes to the surface of the mixture.

4 Add the chic' eggplant and si 8 minutes, ensuring the mixture does not boil. Stir in the lime leaves, fish sauce, palm sugar and lime juice, and cook for another minute. Stir in the Thai basil and garnish with the extra leaves. Serve with steamed rice.

Nutrition per serve: Fat 44 g; Protein 31 g; Carbohydrate 10 g; Dietary Fibre 3.5 g; Cholesterol 82.5 mg; 2320 kJ (555 Cal)

Notes: Any remaining curry paste can be frozen in convenient 1 tablespoon measures in a freezer bag for future use.

For a milder curry, remove the seeds and membrane from the chillies used in the paste.

MACARONI CHEESE

Prep time: 10 minutes
Cooking time: 35 minutes
Serves 6

500 g elbow macaroni
2 cups (500 ml) milk
80 g butter
3 tablespoons plain flour
100 g Cheddar, roughly
   grated
100 g Gruyère, grated
pinch ground nutmeg
60 g Parmesan, finely grated

1 Preheat the oven to moderately hot 200°C (400°F/Gas 6). Cook the macaroni in a large saucepan of boiling water until *al dente*, drain and return to the pan.
2 Meanwhile, heat the milk until it is just simmering. Melt 60 g butter in a saucepan, stir in the flour and cook for 1 minute, or until foaming. Remove from the heat and gradually stir in the hot milk. Return the pan to the heat and stir constantly until the sauce boils and thickens. Reduce the heat and simmer for 2 minutes.
3 Pour the sauce over the macaroni, stir in the Cheddar, Gruyère and nutmeg, and season well. Grease a 1.5 litre ovenproof dish with the remaining butter and pour in the macaroni mixture. Sprinkle with the Parmesan and bake for 20 minutes, or until the top is golden.

Nutrition per serve: Fat 28.5 g; Protein 26 g; Carbohydrate 65 g; Dietary Fibre 3 g; Cholesterol 86 mg; 2600 kJ (620 Cal)

VEGETABLE BAKE

Prep time: 35 minutes +
   10 minutes standing
Cooking time: 1 hour
   25 minutes
Serves 6

4 large unpeeled potatoes,
   halved
600 g unpeeled orange
   sweet potatoes, halved
20 g butter
1 tablespoon olive oil
2 large leeks, thinly sliced
3 cloves garlic, crushed
6 zucchini, thinly sliced on
   the diagonal
300 ml cream
130 g grated Parmesan
1 tablespoon finely chopped
   fresh thyme
1 tablespoon chopped fresh
   flat-leaf parsley
130 g grated Cheddar

1 Preheat the oven to moderate 180°C (350°F/Gas 4) and grease a deep, 2.5 litre ovenproof dish. Boil the potato and sweet potato for 10 minutes. Meanwhile, heat the butter and oil in a frying pan. Add the leek and cook over low heat for 4–5 minutes, or until softened. Add 1 clove garlic and the zucchini, and cook for 3–4 minutes, or until the zucchini starts to soften. Combine the cream, Parmesan, herbs and remaining garlic and season to taste.
2 When the potatoes and sweet potatoes are cool enough to handle, peel off the skins and thinly slice. Layer half the potato slices in the base of the dish. Season. Spread with a quarter of the cream mixture, then cover with the zucchini mixture, patting down well. Top with another quarter of the cream mixture. Use all the sweet potato slices to make another layer, and cover with half of the remaining cream mixture. Top with the remaining potato slices, then the last of the cream mixture. Season and top with the Cheddar.
3 Bake for 1 hour 15 minutes, or until the vegetables are cooked through. Cover with a tented sheet of foil towards the end if the top starts over-browning. Stand for 10 minutes before cutting.

Nutrition per serve: Fat 42.5 g; Protein 20 g; Carbohydrate 31 g; Dietary Fibre 5.5 g; Cholesterol 120.5 mg; 2435 kJ (580 Cal)

Macaroni cheese (top),
and Vegetable bake

CORNED BEEF WITH PARSLEY SAUCE

Prep time: 25 minutes
Cooking time: 2 hours
  10 minutes
Serves 4–6

1.5 kg corned beef
  (silverside)
1 onion, halved
8 whole cloves
2 tablespoons malt vinegar
1 1/2 tablespoons soft brown
  sugar
8 black peppercorns
1 bay leaf
4 potatoes, peeled and
  quartered
335 g baby carrots

Parsley sauce
40 g butter
2 tablespoons plain flour
2 cups (500 ml) milk
1/2 teaspoon mustard
  powder
2 tablespoons chopped
  fresh flat-leaf parsley

1 Place the beef in a very large, heavy-based saucepan and add enough cold water to cover. Slowly bring to the boil, then drain and discard the water. Pour in enough fresh, cold water to just cover the meat in the pan. Stud each half of the onion with the cloves and add to the pan with the vinegar,

Corned beef with
parsley sauce

sugar, peppercorns and bay leaf. Cover the pan and bring the water to a simmer. Cook for 2 hours, or until the meat feels tender when tested in the thickest part with a metal skewer. As the liquid level drops, spoon some over the meat occasionally. Do not allow the liquid to boil or the meat will become tough. Remove the meat from the dish, cover with foil and keep warm. Reserve 1/2 cup (125 ml) of the cooking liquid.

2 Meanwhile, to make the parsley sauce, melt the butter in a saucepan and stir in the flour. Cook, stirring, for 1 minute then remove from the heat. Gradually add the milk and stir until the sauce is smooth. Return to the heat and bring to the boil, stirring continuously. Simmer for 1 minute, then add the mustard powder. Remove the pan from the heat and cover the surface of the sauce with plastic wrap, to prevent a skin forming.

3 Boil the potatoes for 10 minutes, then add the carrots and continue to boil for another 5 minutes, or until tender. Drain and keep hot. Remove the plastic wrap from the sauce, add the reserved cooking liquid and parsley and

season with salt and freshly ground black pepper. Stir the sauce over low heat until heated through.

4 To serve, slice the beef across the grain and divide among warmed serving plates. Arrange the vegetables around the beef. Spoon some of the parsley sauce over the beef and serve the remaining sauce in a jug.

Nutrition per serve (6): Fat 18 g; Protein 45 g; Carbohydrate 25 g; Dietary Fibre 3.5 g; Cholesterol 145 mg; 1850 kJ (440 Cal)

Variation: Add 1 tablespoon small capers to the parsley sauce just before serving.

OGANOFF

minutes

...ng time: 20 minutes
Serves 4

400 g beef fillet, cut into
    1 cm x 5 cm strips
2 tablespoons plain flour
50 g butter
1 onion, thinly sliced
1 clove garlic, crushed
250 g small Swiss brown
    mushrooms, sliced
50 ml brandy
1 cup (250 ml) beef stock
1 1/2 tablespoons tomato
    paste
3/4 cup (185 g) sour cream
1 tablespoon chopped fresh
    flat-leaf parsley

1 Dust the beef strips
in flour, shaking off any
excess.
2 Melt half the butter
in a large frying pan and
cook the meat in small
batches for 1–2 minutes,
or until seared all over.
Remove. Add the
remaining butter to the
pan and cook the onion
and garlic over medium
heat for 2–3 minutes, or
until they soften. Add
the mushrooms and
cook for 2–3 minutes.
Pour in the brandy
and simmer until nearly
all of the liquid has
evaporated, then stir
in the beef stock and
tomato paste. Cook for
5 minutes to reduce the
liquid slightly. Return
the beef strips to the pan
with any juices and stir
in the sour cream.
Simmer for 1 minute, or
until the sauce thickens
slightly. Season to taste
with salt and freshly
ground black pepper.
3 Garnish with the
chopped parsley and
serve immediately with
fettucine or steamed rice.

Nutrition per serve: Fat 32.5 g;
Protein 27 g; Carbohydrate 9 g;
Dietary Fibre 2.5 g; Cholesterol
156 mg; 1860 kJ (445 Cal)

SALMON CAKES

Prep time: 20 minutes +
    30 minutes chilling
Cooking time: 35 minutes
Serves 4

600 g pontiac potatoes,
    peeled and cut in chunks
415 g can salmon, drained
4 spring onions, thinly
    sliced
1 celery stick, finely chopped
1/4 cup (7 g) chopped fresh
    flat-leaf parsley
2 eggs, lightly beaten
1 teaspoon lemon rind
1 tablespoon lemon juice
1/4 cup (60 g) mayonnaise
1/2 cup (60 g) grated
    Cheddar
2 dashes Tabasco sauce
1 egg, extra, lightly beaten
    with 1 tablespoon water
1 cup (80 g) fresh
    breadcrumbs
1/4 cup (60 ml) oil
1 lemon, cut into wedges,
    to serve

1 Boil the potato for
15 minutes, or until
tender, then drain and
allow to cool. Place the
potato in a large bowl,
and mash lightly, leaving
a few chunks. Add the
salmon, spring onion,
celery, parsley, eggs,
lemon rind, lemon juice,
mayonnaise, cheese and
Tabasco sauce. Season,
then mix until the
ingredients are well
combined.
2 Divide the potato
mixture into 8 portions.
Shape each portion into
a 6 cm x 2 cm patty and
place on a baking tray
lined with baking paper,
then chill for 20 minutes.
When the patties are
firm, dip into the egg
and water mixture,
coating well, and drain
off the excess. Coat the
patties in breadcrumbs,
and refrigerate for a
further 10 minutes.
3 Heat the oil in a non-
stick frying pan over
medium–high heat,
and cook the patties
in two batches for
5 minutes each side,
or until golden brown.
Drain well on crumpled
paper towels and serve
with lemon wedges and
a tossed green salad.

Nutrition per serve: Fat 26 g;
Protein 21 g; Carbohydrate 28 g;
Dietary Fibre 3.5 g; Cholesterol
195 mg; 1780 kJ (425 Cal)

Beef stroganoff (top), and
Salmon cakes

MOUSSAKA

Prep time: 30 minutes +
10 minutes standing
Cooking time: 2 hours
35 minutes
Serves 4–6

1.5 kg eggplant, cut into
1 cm slices
1/4 cup (60 ml) olive oil
1 large onion, chopped
3 cloves garlic, finely
chopped
1 teaspoon ground cumin
1/4 teaspoon ground
cinnamon
1.2 kg lamb mince
1/3 cup (90 g) tomato paste
1 cup (250 ml) red wine
2 x 425 g cans diced
tomatoes
1 tablespoon chopped fresh
oregano
2 tablespoons chopped
fresh flat-leaf parsley
100 g butter
3/4 cup (90 g) plain flour
3 cups (750 ml) milk
1/4 teaspoon ground nutmeg
3/4 cup (75 g) grated
kefalotyri cheese (see Note)
3 eggs, lightly beaten

1 Lightly grease a 3 litre
ceramic ovenproof dish
and preheat the grill to
hot. Place the eggplant
slices on an oiled baking
tray, brush lightly with
2 tablespoons oil and grill
for 5–7 minutes each side,
or until browned. Grill
the rest of the eggplant,
in batches if necessary.

Moussaka

2 Preheat the oven
to moderate 180°C
(350°F/Gas 4). Heat
the remaining tablespoon
of oil in a large saucepan.
Add the onion and cook
over medium heat for
5 minutes, or until
brown. Add the garlic,
cumin and cinnamon,
and cook for a further
minute. Increase the
heat to high, add the
mince and cook for
5 minutes, or until
the meat has browned,
breaking up any lumps
with a fork. Drain off
any oil.

3 Add the tomato paste
and cook for 2 minutes.
Pour in the wine, reduce
the heat and simmer
for 5 minutes, or until
reduced by half. Add
the tomato, oregano
and parsley, and simmer
over medium heat for
1 hour, or until nearly
all of the liquid has
evaporated.

4 Meanwhile, melt the
butter in a saucepan. Stir
in the flour and cook
for 1 minute, or until
foaming. Remove from
the heat and gradually
stir in the milk and
nutmeg. Return to the
heat and stir constantly
until the sauce boils and
thickens. Reduce the
heat and simmer for two
minutes. Stir in 1/2 cup
(50 g) cheese, then
remove from the heat
and stir in the eggs just
before using.

5 To asse
moussaka,
of the egg,
across the
dish and to
of the minc_ ...ixture.
Layer another third
of the eggplant into
the dish, and spread the
remaining mince across
the top. Finish with a
layer of eggplant, then
top with the white
sauce. Sprinkle with the
remaining cheese and
bake for 35 minutes,
or until evenly browned.
Leave for 10 minutes
before serving.

Nutrition per serve (6): Fat 48 g;
Protein 59 g; Carbohydrate 34 g;
Dietary Fibre 9.5 g; Cholesterol
309.5 mg; 3445 kJ (820 Cal)

Note: Kefalotyri is a very hard
Greek cheese made from sheep
or goat's milk. The taste and
texture are similar to Parmesan
cheese, and Parmesan or
pecorino can be used instead.

BEEF SALAD

Prep time: 30 minutes +
15 minutes refrigeration
Cooking time: 10 minutes
Serves 4

1 tablespoon oil
2 x 250 g pieces rump steak
3 1/2 tablespoons lime juice
2 tablespoons fish sauce
1 teaspoon grated palm
   sugar
2 cloves garlic, crushed
1 stem lemon grass, white
   part only, finely sliced
2 small fresh red chillies,
   finely sliced
4 red Asian shallots, finely
   sliced
15–20 fresh mint leaves
1/2 cup (15 g) fresh coriander
   leaves
125 g cherry tomatoes,
   halved
1 Lebanese cucumber,
   halved lengthways and
   thinly sliced
3 cups (180 g) shredded
   Chinese cabbage
1/4 cup (20 g) prepared
   Asian fried onions
1 tablespoon prepared Asian
   fried garlic
1/4 cup (40 g) crushed
   peanuts, to garnish

1 Heat the oil in a large,
non-stick frying pan over
high heat. Cook the steak
for 4 minutes each side,
then remove and cool.
2 Combine the lime
juice, fish sauce, palm
sugar, garlic, lemon grass
and chilli and stir to
dissolve the sugar. Add
the shallots, mint and
coriander. Thinly slice
the beef across the grain,
and toss through the
mixture. Chill for
15 minutes. Add the
tomato and cucumber
and toss. Arrange the
cabbage on a serving
platter and top with the
beef mixture. Sprinkle
with the fried onion,
garlic and peanuts.

Nutrition per serve: Fat 11 g;
Protein 32 g; Carbohydrate 5 g;
Dietary Fibre 3.5 g; Cholesterol
80 mg; 1040 kJ (250 Cal)

FISH AND CHIPS

Prep time: 15 minutes +
   30 minutes standing
Cooking time: 35 minutes
Serves 4

2 cups (250 g) self-raising
   flour
1 cup (250 ml) beer
4 large desiree or King
   Edward potatoes, peeled
oil, for deep-frying
4 firm white fish fillets (200 g
   each), skinned, boned and
   cut into 3 even pieces
seasoned plain flour, for
   dusting
lemon wedges, to serve

1 Sift the self-raising
flour and 1 teaspoon
salt into a bowl and
make a well in the
centre. Slowly add the
beer and 1 cup (250 ml)
water, whisking to make
a smooth batter. Cover
and leave for 30 minutes.
2 Meanwhile, cut the
potatoes into 1 cm thick
chips. Soak the chips in
a bowl of cold water for
10 minutes, then dry
with paper towels. Fill
a heavy-based saucepan
one-third full of oil and
heat to 160°C (315°F)
or until a cube of bread
browns in 30 seconds.
Cook the chips in
batches for 3–5 minutes,
or until they are pale and
golden. Remove and
drain on paper towels.
3 Reheat the oil to
180°C (350°F), or until
a cube of bread browns
in 15 seconds. Cook the
batches of chips for
another 2–3 minutes,
or until crisp. Drain and
keep hot on a baking tray
in the oven. Lower the
oil temperature to 170°C
(375°F) or until a cube
of bread browns in
20 seconds.
4 Lightly coat the fish
in flour, shaking off any
excess, then dip in the
batter. Cook in batches
for 4 minutes, or until
golden and the fish is
cooked through. Drain
on paper towels. Season
and serve with the chips
and lemon.

Nutrition per serve: Fat 33 g;
Protein 51 g; Carbohydrate 69 g;
Dietary Fibre 5 g; Cholesterol
118 mg; 3340 kJ (800 Cal)

Thai beef salad (top),
and Fish and chips

CHICKEN POT PIES

Prep time: 30 minutes +
  1 hour 30 minutes
  refrigeration
Cooking time: 1 hour
Serves 4

Pastry
150 g plain flour
100 g chilled butter, cut
  into cubes
1/4 cup (60 g) sour cream
1 egg yolk, mixed with
  1 teaspoon milk, to glaze

Filling
125 g fresh or frozen peas
1 tablespoon olive oil
600 g chicken tenderloins,
  trimmed and cut into
  2 cm pieces
50 g butter
1 large leek, white part only,
  sliced
2 bacon rashers, chopped
2 tablespoons plain flour
1 cup (250 ml) chicken stock
1/3 cup (80 ml) thick cream
1 egg yolk
2 tablespoons snipped fresh
  chives

1 Sift the flour into a large bowl and add the butter. Rub the butter into the flour with your fingertips until the mixture resembles fine breadcrumbs, then stir in the sour cream. Add enough iced water to form a soft dough, using a flat-bladed knife to mix it in with a cutting,

Chicken pot pies

rather than a stirring action. Turn the dough out onto a lightly floured surface and gather it together into a smooth ball. Do not knead or the pastry will become tough. Cover with plastic wrap and chill for 1 hour.

2 Roll the pastry out on a lightly floured surface to 2 mm thick. Cut out four 14 cm diameter circles, carefully lift the rounds onto a lightly floured baking tray, cover and chill for 30 minutes. Preheat the oven to hot 220° C (425°F/Gas 7).

3 Blanch the peas in a small saucepan of boiling water for 5 minutes, or until just tender. Heat the oil in a large frying pan over high heat, and lightly brown the chicken in batches. Remove from the pan.

4 Melt the butter in the same frying pan over medium heat, and cook the leek and bacon for 5 minutes, or until the leek is soft and the bacon is lightly browned. Stir in the flour and continue to cook for 1 minute, or until lightly browned. Gradually add the stock, stirring vigorously to remove any lumps, and cook for 5–6 minutes, or until the sauce starts to boil and thicken. Return the chicken and peas to the pan, and simmer for 5 minutes,

or until the s[...] thickens and [...] is cooked thr[...]

5 Combine [...] egg yolk and chives, and add to the sauce. Stir until the sauce is slightly thickened, but do not let it come to the boil or it will curdle. Divide the chicken mixture among four 1 cup (250 ml) ceramic ovenproof dishes, being careful not to overfill. Brush the edges of the pastry with the egg glaze and cover each pot, pressing to secure the pastry to the dish. Brush with the egg glaze, make a small slit in the top to allow steam to escape, and bake for 20 minutes, or until the pastry is golden. Serve with crusty bread and a green salad, if desired.

Nutrition per serve: Fat 58 g;
Protein 42 g; Carbohydrate 28 g;
Dietary Fibre 3.5 g; Cholesterol
339 mg; 3325 kJ (795 Cal)

VF

~~GET~~ABLE AND ~~N~~OODLE STIR-FRY

Prep time: 25 minutes
Cooking time: 10 minutes
Serves 4

350 g fresh hokkien noodles
1 teaspoon sesame oil
2 tablespoons vegetable oil
1 red onion, halved and
    thinly sliced
3 cloves garlic, crushed
3 cm x 3 cm piece fresh
    ginger, julienned
5 spring onions, cut into
    5 cm lengths
1 small fresh red chilli,
    seeded and finely chopped
3 star anise
1 small red capsicum, finely
    sliced
100 g snow peas, trimmed
    and halved diagonally
100 g cap mushrooms,
    quartered
500 g baby bok choy,
    trimmed, leaves separated,
    cut into 5 cm lengths
115 g baby corn, halved
    diagonally
2 teaspoons cornflour
100 ml Chinese barbecue
    sauce (char sui)
2 tablespoons Chinese rice
    wine
1/2 cup (15 g) fresh coriander
    leaves

1 Place the noodles in a large heatproof bowl, cover with boiling water and leave to soak for 5 minutes. Use a fork to gently separate the noodles and drain well. Toss with the sesame oil.

2 Heat a wok over high heat. Add the vegetable oil and swirl to coat. Add the red onion, garlic, ginger, spring onion and chilli, and stir-fry for 1 minute. Add the star anise, capsicum, snow peas, mushrooms, bok choy and baby corn and stir-fry for 2–3 minutes.

3 Mix the cornflour with 1 teaspoon cold water. Add to the wok with the barbecue sauce and Chinese wine. Bring to the boil and cook for 1 minute, or until the ingredients are coated and the sauce thickens slightly. Toss in the coriander leaves and serve immediately.

Nutrition per serve: Fat 12.5 g; Protein 14 g; Carbohydrate 69 g; Dietary Fibre 7.5 g; Cholesterol 11.5 mg; 1880 kJ (450 Cal)

SNAPPER WITH CAPER AND LEMON BUTTER SAUCE

Prep time: 10 minutes
Cooking time: 25 minutes
Serves 4

1/4 cup (60 ml) chicken stock
1/4 cup (60 ml) lemon juice
200 g butter, chilled and
    diced
3 teaspoons baby capers
10 g butter, extra
4 snapper fillets, skin on
    (about 180 g each)

1 Pour the stock and lemon juice into a small saucepan and bring to the boil. Reduce the heat and simmer for 2–3 minutes, or until reduced to 2 tablespoons. Whisk in the butter a few pieces at a time. Do not allow the sauce to boil. If it becomes too hot, lift off the heat for a moment while whisking in the butter. The sauce will thicken as the butter is added until it has a creamy consistency. Stir in the capers and season to taste with pepper.

2 Melt the extra butter in a large frying pan and cook the snapper fillets over medium–high heat for 2–3 minutes on each side, or until the flesh flakes easily when tested with a fork. If the fillets are very large, you may need to cook them in two batches.

3 Spoon the sauce over the fish and serve with steamed vegetables.

Nutrition per serve: Fat 45.5 g; Protein 37 g; Carbohydrate 1 g; Dietary Fibre 0 g; Cholesterol 242.5 mg; 2335 kJ (560 Cal)

Vegetable and noodle stir-fry
(top), and Snapper
with caper and
lemon butter sauce

LAMB KORMA WITH SAFFRON RICE

Prep time: 25 minutes +
   1 hour marinating +
   30 minutes soaking
Cooking time: 1 hour
   25 minutes
Serves 4–6

2 kg leg of lamb, boned
1 onion, chopped
2 teaspoons grated fresh
   ginger
3 cloves garlic, peeled
2 teaspoons ground
   coriander
2 teaspoons ground cumin
1 teaspoon cardamom
   seeds
large pinch cayenne pepper
2 tablespoons ghee or oil
1 onion, sliced, extra
1/2 cup (125 g) plain yoghurt
1/2 cup (125 ml) thick cream
1 cinnamon stick
1/2 cup (50 g) ground
   almonds
toasted slivered almonds,
   to garnish
fresh coriander leaves,
   to garnish

Saffron rice
2 cups (400 g) basmati rice
25 g butter
3 bay leaves
1/4 teaspoon saffron threads
2 cups (500 ml) boiling
   vegetable stock

1 Trim any excess fat or sinew from the lamb, cut into 3 cm cubes and place in a large bowl. Put the onion, ginger, garlic, coriander, cumin, cardamom seeds, cayenne pepper and 1/2 teaspoon salt in a food processor, and process to a smooth paste. Add the spice mixture to the lamb and mix well to coat. Leave to marinate for 1 hour.
2 Heat the ghee in a large saucepan, add the extra onion and cook, stirring, over low heat for 7 minutes, or until the onion is soft. Add the lamb mixture to the pan in batches and cook, stirring constantly, for 8 minutes, or until the lamb changes colour. Return all the lamb to the pan, add the yoghurt, cream, cinnamon stick and ground almonds, and stir until combined.
3 Reduce the heat, cover, and simmer, stirring occasionally, for 50 minutes, or until the meat is tender. Add a little water if the mixture becomes too dry. Season to taste.
4 Meanwhile, to make the saffron rice, wash the basmati rice thoroughly, cover with cold water and soak for 30 minutes. Drain. Melt the butter gently in a large, deep frying pan, add the bay leaves and washed rice, and cook, stirring, for 6 minutes, or until all the moisture has evaporated. Soak saffron in 2 tablespoon hot water for 2 minutes. Add the saffron and its soaking liquid to the rice with the stock and 1 1/2 cups (375 ml) boiling water, and season to taste. Bring to the boil, then reduce the heat to low and cook, covered, for 12–15 minutes, or until all the water is absorbed and the rice is cooked.
5 Serve the korma with the rice, and garnish with the slivered almonds and coriander leaves.

Nutrition per serve (6): Fat 32 g; Protein 37 g; Carbohydrate 59 g; Dietary Fibre 2.5 g; Cholesterol 126.5 mg; 2800 kJ (670 Cal)

Note: Korma curries can also be made using beef or chicken. Korma refers to the style of curry — rich and smooth, and including almonds.

Lamb korma with saffron rice

CHICKEN CASSEROLE WITH MUSTARD AND TARRAGON

Prep time: 15 minutes
Cooking time: 1 hour
　30 minutes
Serves 4–6

1/4 cup (60 ml) olive oil
1 kg chicken thigh fillets, halved, then quartered
1 onion, finely chopped
1 leek, sliced
1 clove garlic, finely chopped
350 g button mushrooms, sliced
1/2 teaspoon dried tarragon
1 1/2 cups (375 ml) chicken stock
3/4 cup (185 ml) cream
2 teaspoons lemon juice
2 teaspoons Dijon mustard

1 Preheat the oven to moderate 180°C (350°F/ Gas 4). Heat 1 tablespoon of the oil in a flameproof casserole dish over medium heat, and cook the chicken in two batches for 6–7 minutes each, or until golden. Remove from the dish.

2 Add the remaining oil to the casserole dish and cook the onion, leek and garlic over medium heat for 5 minutes, or until soft. Add the mushrooms and cook for 5–7 minutes, or until they are soft and browned, and most of the liquid has evaporated. Add the tarragon, chicken stock, cream, lemon juice and mustard, bring to the boil and cook for 2 minutes. Return the chicken pieces to the dish and season well. Cover.

3 Place the casserole in the oven and cook for 1 hour, or until the sauce has reduced and thickened. Season to taste with salt and pepper, and serve with potatoes and a green salad.

Nutrition per serve (6): Fat 51 g; Protein 53 g; Carbohydrate 6 g; Dietary Fibre 3.5 g; Cholesterol 282.5 mg; 2855 kJ (685 Cal)

BEEF IN BLACK BEAN SAUCE

Prep time: 20 minutes
Cooking time: 10 minutes
Serves 4

4 tablespoons canned salted black beans in soy sauce
750 g rump steak
1 tablespoon peanut oil
1 tablespoon sesame oil
1 large onion, thinly sliced
1 clove garlic, finely chopped
4 cm x 1 cm piece of fresh ginger, peeled and finely chopped
1 small fresh red chilli, finely chopped
2 teaspoons cornflour
2 tablespoons dark soy sauce
1 teaspoon sugar
1/4 cup (60 ml) beef stock
1 spring onion, thinly sliced on the diagonal, to garnish

1 Rinse and then soak the black beans in cold water for 5 minutes. Drain and roughly mash the beans with a fork. Trim the steak of all fat and sinew, then cut the meat in thin slices across the grain.

2 Heat a wok over high heat, add half each of the peanut and sesame oils, and swirl to coat. Add the beef in two batches, and stir-fry for 2 minutes or until well browned. Remove the beef and any liquid to a bowl. Heat the remaining oils, add the onion and stir-fry for 2 minutes. Add the garlic, ginger and chilli, and continue to stir-fry for 1 minute.

3 Mix the cornflour with 1 teaspoon water, then return the beef and any cooking liquid to the wok with the black beans, soy sauce, sugar, stock and cornflour paste. Stir-fry for 1–2 minutes, or until the sauce boils and thickens. Garnish with the spring onions and serve with steamed rice.

Nutrition per serve: Fat 18.5 g; Protein 43 g; Carbohydrate 10 g; Dietary Fibre 1.5 g; Cholesterol 121 mg; 1585 kJ (380 Cal)

Chicken casserole with mustard and tarragon (top), and Beef in black bean sauce

VEGETABLE LASAGNE

Prep time: 40 minutes +
   30 minutes standing
Cooking time: 1 hour
   15 minutes
Serves 6–8

700 g eggplant, cut
   lengthways into thin slices
1/2 cup (125 ml) olive oil
1 large onion, finely chopped
3 cloves garlic, crushed
300 g small zucchini, cut
   into thin slices
300 g button mushrooms,
   sliced
pinch dried chilli flakes
1/4 teaspoon ground nutmeg
400 g can diced tomatoes
8 fresh basil leaves, torn
200 g fresh lasagne sheets,
   or 150 g dried sheets
750 g ricotta
1/3 cup (80 ml) cream
1 egg, lightly beaten
100 g grated reggiano
   Parmesan
400 g coarsely grated
   mozzarella
3 tablespoons pine nuts

1 Sprinkle the eggplant slices with salt and place in a colander to drain for 20 minutes. Meanwhile, heat 2 tablespoons oil in a large, deep frying pan and cook the onion over low heat for 6–8 minutes, or until softened but not brown. Stir in the garlic, zucchini, mushrooms, chilli flakes and half the nutmeg, and cook over medium–high heat for 4–5 minutes, or until the vegetables start to brown. Add the tomato, basil and 1 cup (250 ml) water, and season with salt and freshly ground black pepper. Reduce the heat and simmer for 10 minutes, increasing the heat towards the end of cooking if necessary, to give a thick sauce.

2 Preheat the grill to high. Rinse the eggplant slices in cold water and pat them dry with paper towels. Brush well on both sides with oil and grill in batches for 2–3 minutes each side, or until browned.

3 If you are using dried lasagne sheets, cook them, a few at a time, in boiling water until *al dente*. Transfer to a bowl of cold water, then spread on clean, dry tea towels to drain. Combine the ricotta, cream, egg, remaining nutmeg and half the Parmesan in a bowl, and season well with salt and ground black pepper.

4 Preheat the oven to moderate 180°C (350°F/ Gas 4), and grease a 30 cm x 21 cm deep-sided ovenproof dish. Spread half the tomato sauce over the base of the dish. Sprinkle with a third of the mozzarella, then cover this with a layer of lasagne sheets, slightly overlapping. Spread half the ricotta filling over the pasta. Layer all of the eggplant slices over the ricotta. Spread with the rest of the sauce, then another layer of the lasagne sheets. Top with the remaining ricotta and sprinkle the pine nuts over the surface. Cover with the remaining mozzarella and sprinkle with the last of the grated Parmesan.

5 Bake for 35 minutes, or until the lasagne has puffed up and the cheese is golden. Turn the oven off, prop the door ajar and let the lasagne rest for 10 minutes before serving.

Nutrition per serve (8): Fat 48 g;
Protein 34 g; Carbohydrate 22 g;
Dietary Fibre 5.5 g; Cholesterol
102 mg; 2705 kJ (645 Cal)

Vegetable lasagne

IRISH STEW

Prep time: 30 minutes
Cooking time: 1 hour
40 minutes
Serves 4

20 g butter
1 tablespoon vegetable oil
8 lamb neck chops, trimmed
4 bacon rashers, cut into
strips
1 teaspoon plain flour
600 g potatoes, peeled and
cut into thick slices
3 carrots, cut into thick slices
1 onion, cut into 16 wedges
1 small leek, cut into thick
slices
150 g savoy cabbage, thinly
sliced
2 cups (500 ml) beef stock
2 tablespoons finely
chopped fresh flat-leaf
parsley

1 Heat the butter and oil in a flameproof casserole dish or a large, heavy-based saucepan over high heat. Add the chops and sauté for 1–2 minutes on each side, or until browned, then remove from the dish. Add the bacon and cook 2–3 minutes, or until crisp. Remove with a slotted spoon, leaving the drippings in the dish.
2 Sprinkle the flour into the dish, and stir to combine. Remove from the heat and layer half the potato, carrot, onion, leek, cabbage and bacon in the base of the dish. Arrange the chops in a single layer over the bacon and cover with layers of the remaining vegetables and bacon.
3 Pour in enough of the stock to cover, then bring to the boil over high heat. Reduce the heat, cover, and simmer for 1 1/2 hours, or until the meat is very tender and the sauce is slightly reduced. Season well with salt and freshly ground black pepper, and serve sprinkled with chopped parsley.

Nutrition per serve: Fat 23.5 g;
Protein 52 g; Carbohydrate 27 g;
Dietary Fibre 6 g; Cholesterol
157 mg; 2200 kJ (525 Cal)

CURRIED SAUSAGES

Prep time: 10 minutes +
15 minutes cooling
Cooking time: 40 minutes
Serves 6

9 thick beef or pork
sausages
1 tablespoon vegetable oil
20 g butter
2 teaspoons grated fresh
ginger
3 cloves garlic, crushed
2 large onions, sliced
3 teaspoons curry powder
1 teaspoon garam masala
2 teaspoons tomato paste
1 tablespoon plain flour
2 1/2 cups (625 ml) hot
chicken stock
2 bay leaves

1 Place the sausages in a saucepan, cover with cold water and bring to the boil. Lower the heat and simmer for 3 minutes. Remove from the heat and allow to cool in the water, then drain, pat dry, and cut into 2 cm pieces.
2 Heat the oil in a large frying pan over high heat, and cook the sausages for 2–3 minutes, or until golden all over. Drain on paper towels.
3 Using the same pan, melt the butter, then add the ginger, garlic and onion. Cook over medium heat for about 5 minutes, or until the onion is soft and golden. Add the curry powder and garam masala, and cook for 1 minute, or until fragrant. Stir in the tomato paste, and cook for 1 minute, then add the flour. Stir to combine, then gradually pour in the stock, taking care that no lumps form. Bring to a simmer, add the bay leaves and the sausages, and cook over low heat for 15 minutes, or until thickened. Season and serve with mashed potato.

Nutrition per serve: Fat 34 g;
Protein 16 g; Carbohydrate 9 g;
Dietary Fibre 4.5 g; Cholesterol
64 mg; 1665 kJ (400 Cal)

Irish stew (top), and
Curried sausages

BEEF NACHOS

Prep time: 25 minutes
Cooking time: 30 minutes
Serves 4

2 tablespoons oil
1 onion, chopped
2 cloves garlic, crushed
1 tablespoon ground cumin
3 teaspoons ground
   coriander
1 teaspoon chilli powder
400 g lean beef mince
1 1/2 cups (375 g) bottled
   tomato pasta sauce
425 g can refried beans
230 g packet plain corn
   chips
2 cups (250 g) grated
   Cheddar, at room
   temperature
150 g sour cream
4 spring onions, green parts
   included, sliced
fresh coriander leaves,
   to garnish

Guacamole
2 large, ripe avocados
1/2 small onion, grated
1 clove garlic, crushed
1 tomato, peeled, seeded
   and diced
1 tablespoon lime juice
2 tablespoons chopped
   fresh coriander

1 Preheat the oven to moderate 180°C (350°F/Gas 4). Heat the oil in a large frying pan over medium heat and cook the chopped onion, garlic, cumin, ground coriander and chilli powder for 2–3 minutes. Add the mince and cook over high heat for about 3–4 minutes, or until well browned, breaking up any lumps with a fork. Stir in the tomato pasta sauce and refried beans, and simmer for 8–10 minutes, or until the mixture thickens.

2 Meanwhile, to make the guacamole, cut the avocados in half and remove the stones. Scoop out the flesh, place in a small bowl and mash roughly with a fork. Add the grated onion, crushed garlic, tomato, lime juice, chopped coriander and 1/4 teaspoon salt, and stir until well combined.

3 Divide the corn chips among 4 ovenproof serving plates, arranging them close together, with a slight well in the centre. Place in the oven for 8–10 minutes, or until the corn chips are hot and golden. Remove from the oven and sprinkle immediately with the grated cheese (the heat from the chips will melt the cheese). Spoon equal quantities of the beef mixture into the well of each pile of chips. Top with the guacamole and sour cream, and sprinkle with the spring onion. Garnish with fresh coriander leaves and serve.

Beef nachos

Nutrition per serve: Fat 93.5 g;
Protein 53 g; Carbohydrate 57 g;
Dietary Fibre 17.5 g; Cholesterol
164.5 mg; 5295 kJ (1265 Cal)

Note: 1–2 fresh Jalapeño or serrano chillies, seeded and finely chopped, can be added to give a bite to the guacamole.

For a vegetarian option, omit the beef and start by cooking the onion, garlic and spices. Add a 440 g can of red kidney beans, drained and rinsed, with the pasta sauce and simmer for 8–10 minutes. Continue with the rest of the recipe and serve.

BAKED RICE PUDDING

Prep time: 10 minutes +
 5 minutes standing
Cooking time: 1 hour
Serves 4–6

20 g unsalted butter, melted
3 tablespoons short-grain
 rice
3 eggs
1/4 cup (60 g) caster sugar
13/4 cups (440 ml) milk
1/2 cup (125 ml) cream
1 teaspoon vanilla essence
1/4 teaspoon ground nutmeg

1 Preheat the oven to warm 160°C (315°F/ Gas 2–3) and brush a 1.5 litre ovenproof dish with melted butter. Cook the rice in a saucepan of boiling water for 12 minutes, or until tender, then drain well.

2 Place the eggs in a bowl and beat lightly. Add the sugar, milk, cream and vanilla, and whisk until well combined. Stir in the cooked rice, pour into the prepared dish and sprinkle with nutmeg.

3 Place the dish in a deep roasting tin and pour enough hot water into the tin to come halfway up the side of the pudding dish. Bake for 45 minutes, or until the custard is lightly set and a knife inserted into the centre comes out clean. Remove the pudding dish from the roasting tin and leave for 5 minutes before serving. Serve the pudding with poached or stewed fruit.

Nutrition per serve (6): Fat 18 g; Protein 7 g; Carbohydrate 20 g; Dietary Fibre 0 g; Cholesterol 148.5 mg; 1080 kJ (260 Cal)

Variation: Add 2 tablespoons of sultanas or chopped, dried apricots to the custard mixture before baking.

LEMON DELICIOUS

Prep time: 25 minutes +
 5 minutes standing
Cooking time: 55 minutes
Serves 4–6

70 g unsalted butter, at room
 temperature
3/4 cup (185 g) sugar
2 teaspoons finely grated
 lemon rind
3 eggs, separated
1/4 cup (30 g) self-raising
 flour
3/4 cup (185 ml) milk
1/3 cup (80 ml) lemon juice
icing sugar, to serve
thick cream, to serve

1 Preheat the oven to moderate 180°C (350°F/ Gas 4). Melt 10 g of the butter and use to lightly grease a 1.25 litre ovenproof ceramic dish. Using an electric beater, beat the remaining butter, the sugar and grated rind together in a bowl until the mixture is light and creamy.

2 Gradually add the egg yolks, beating well after each addition. Fold in the flour and milk alternately to make a smooth, but runny batter. Stir in the lemon juice. Don't worry if the batter looks like it has separated at this stage.

3 Whisk the egg whites in a clean, dry bowl until firm peaks form and, with a large metal spoon, fold a third of the whites into the batter. Gently fold in the remaining egg whites, being careful not to overmix. Pour the batter into the prepared dish, and place in a large roasting tin. Pour enough hot water into the tin to come one-third of the way up the side of the dish and bake for 55 minutes or until the top of the pudding is golden, risen and firm to the touch. Leave for 5 minutes before serving. Dust with icing sugar and serve with cream.

Nutrition per serve (6): Fat 13 g; Protein 6 g; Carbohydrate 33 g; Dietary Fibre 0.5 g; Cholesterol 130.5 mg; 1075 kJ (255 Cal)

Baked rice pudding (top), and Lemon delicious

BREAD AND BUTTER PUDDING

Prep time: 15 minutes +
 5 minutes standing
Cooking time: 30 minutes
Serves 4

50 g unsalted butter
8 thick slices day-old white
 bread
1 teaspoon ground
 cinnamon
2 tablespoons sultanas
3 eggs
1 egg yolk
3 tablespoons caster sugar
1 cup (250 ml) milk
2 cups (500 ml) cream
1/2 teaspoon vanilla essence
1 tablespoon demerara
 sugar

1 Preheat the oven to moderate 180°C (350°F/ Gas 4). Melt 10 g of the butter and use to brush a 1.5 litre ovenproof dish. Spread the bread very lightly with the remaining butter and cut each slice in half diagonally. Layer the bread in the prepared dish, sprinkling the cinnamon and sultanas between each layer.
2 Lightly whisk together the eggs, egg yolk and caster sugar in a large bowl. Heat the milk with the cream until just warm and stir in the vanilla. Whisk the cream mixture into the egg mixture. Strain the custard over the layered bread, then leave for 5 minutes before sprinkling with the demerara sugar.
3 Bake for 30 minutes, or until the custard has set and the bread is golden brown. Serve warm or at room temperature.

Nutrition per serve: Fat 73 g;
Protein 18 g; Carbohydrate 65 g;
Dietary Fibre 3 g; Cholesterol
403.5 mg; 4060 kJ (970 Cal)

RHUBARB AND BERRY CRUMBLE

Prep time: 25 minutes +
 5 minutes standing
Cooking time: 35 minutes
Serves 4

10 g butter, to grease
850 g rhubarb, cut into
 2.5 cm lengths
150 g blackberries
1 teaspoon grated orange
 rind
1 cup (250 g) caster sugar
1 cup (125 g) plain flour
1 cup (115 g) ground
 almonds
1/2 teaspoon ground ginger
150 g chilled unsalted butter,
 cubed

1 Preheat the oven to moderate 180°C (350°F/ Gas 4), and grease a deep, 1.5 litre ovenproof dish.

Bring a saucepan or water to the boil over high heat, add the rhubarb, and cook for 2 minutes, or until just tender. Drain well and combine with the berries, orange rind and 1/3 cup (90 g) caster sugar. Taste and add a little more sugar if needed. Spoon the fruit mixture into the prepared dish.
2 To make the topping, combine the flour, ground almonds, ginger and the remaining sugar. Rub the butter into the flour mixture with your fingertips until it resembles coarse breadcrumbs. Sprinkle the crumble mix over the fruit, pressing lightly. Don't press it down too firmly, or it will become flat and dense.
3 Place the dish on a baking tray and bake for 25–30 minutes or until the topping is golden and the fruit is bubbling underneath. Leave for 5 minutes before serving with cream or vanilla ice cream.

Nutrition per serve: Fat 46.5 g;
Protein 11 g; Carbohydrate 84 g;
Dietary Fibre 8.5 g; Cholesterol
97.5 mg; 3285 kJ (785 Cal)

Note: Substitute raspberries,
loganberries or blueberries for
the blackberries. Strawberries
do not work well as they become
too soft when cooked.

Bread and butter pudding
(top), and Rhubarb and
berry crumble

10 g unsalted butter, melted
50 g unsalted butter,
  chopped, extra
75 g good-quality dark
  chocolate, chopped
1/2 cup (125 ml) milk
1 cup (125 g) self-raising
  flour
4 tablespoons cocoa
  powder
2/3 cup (160 g) caster sugar
1 egg, lightly beaten
1/2 cup (115 g) soft brown
  sugar
icing sugar, to dust

1 Preheat the oven to moderate 180°C (350°F/ Gas 4) and lightly grease a 2 litre ovenproof dish with the melted butter. Place the chopped butter, chocolate and milk in a small saucepan, and stir over medium heat for 3–4 minutes, or until the butter and chocolate have melted. Remove the pan from the heat and allow to cool slightly.

2 Sift together the flour and 2 tablespoons of cocoa, and add to the chocolate mixture with the caster sugar and the egg, stirring until just combined. Spoon into the prepared dish.

3 Sift the remaining cocoa evenly over the top of the pudding and sprinkle with the brown sugar. Pour 2 1/4 cups (560 ml) boiling water over the back of a spoon (this stops the water making big holes in the cake mixture) over the top of the pudding. Bake for 40 minutes, or until the pudding is firm to the touch. Leave for 2 minutes before dusting with icing sugar. Serve with cream or vanilla ice cream.

Nutrition per serve: Fat 13 g; Protein 6 g; Carbohydrate 63 g; Dietary Fibre 1.5 g; Cholesterol 58 mg; 1615 kJ (385 Cal)

BAKED CUSTARD

Prep time: 5 minutes +
  10 minutes standing
Cooking time: 35 minutes
Serves 4

10 g butter, melted
3 eggs
1/3 cup (90 g) caster sugar
2 cups (500 ml) milk
1/2 cup (125 ml) cream
1 1/2 teaspoons vanilla
  essence
ground nutmeg

1 Preheat the oven to warm 160°C (315°F/ Gas 2–3) and brush four 1 cup (250 ml) ramekins or a 1.5 litre ovenproof dish with the melted butter. Whisk together the eggs and sugar in a large bowl, until they are combined. Place the milk and cream in a small saucepan and stir over medium heat for 3–4 minutes, or until the mixture is warmed through, then stir into the egg mixture with the vanilla essence. Strain into the prepared dishes and sprinkle with the ground nutmeg.

2 Place the dishes in a deep roasting tin and add enough hot water to come halfway up the side of the dishes. Bake for 25 minutes for the individual custards, or 30 minutes for the large custard, or until it is set and a knife inserted into the centre comes out clean.

3 Remove the custards from the roasting tin and leave for 10 minutes before serving.

Nutrition per serve: Fat 25.5 g; Protein 11 g; Carbohydrate 26 g; Dietary Fibre 0 g; Cholesterol 218.5 mg; 1470 kJ (353 Cal)

Variation: Omit the vanilla and add 1 1/2 tablespoons of Amaretto or Grand Marnier liqueur to the custard before baking.

Self-saucing chocolate pudding (top), and Baked custard

Index